Bridges

Chris Oxlade

Heinemann Library
Chicago, Illinois

© 2001 Reed Educational & Professional Publishing
Published by Heinemann Library,
an imprint of Reed Educational & Professional Publishing,
Chicago, IL
Customer Service 888-454-2279
Visit our website at www.heinemannlibrary.com

Designed by Celia Floyd
Illustrations by Barry Atkinson
Originated by Repro Multi Warna
Printed by Wing King Tong in Hong Kong

05 04 03 02
10 9 8 7 6 5 4 3 2

Library of Congress Cataloging-in-Publication Data

Oxlade, Chris.
    Bridges / Chris Oxlade.
      p. cm. – (Building amazing structures)
    Includes bibliographical references and index.
    Summary: Describes bridges throughout the world, discussing materials and building technologies, functions and locations of important bridges, and examples of famous bridges in history.
    ISBN 1-57572-275-5 (lib. binding)
    1. Bridges—Juvenile literature. [1. Bridges.] I. Series.

TG148 .O94 2000
624′.2—dc21   00-026987

Acknowledgments
The Publishers would like to thank the following for permission to reproduce photographs:
Tony Stone, p. 4; Robert Harding, pp. 5, 28; Eye Ubiquitous/Jonas Grau, p. 6; Eye Ubiquitous/Paul Thomspon, p. 7; Eye Ubiquitous/Judyth Platt, p. 9; Eye Ubiquitous/Michael George, p. 11; Hutchison Library, p. 12; Collections/Brian Shuel, pp. 14, 24, 25; Taylor Woodrow, p. 16; Eye Ubiquitous/David Cumming, p. 17; Eye Ubiquitous/Kevin Wilton, p. 18; Collections/Richard Davis, pp. 20, 21; Eye Ubiquitous/John Wender, p. 23; Associated Press/Chiaki Tsukumo, p. 26; Sund & Baelt, p. 29.

Cover photograph reproduced with permission of Robert Harding Picture Library.

Some words are shown in bold, **like this.** You can find out what they mean by looking in the glossary.

Contents

About Bridges

A bridge is a structure that supports vehicles and people as they cross over an obstacle, such as a road, railroad, or river. It supports their weight and carries it down into the ground at either end of the bridge. We take bridges for granted, but think about how tricky traveling by car or train would be without them.

A structure is a thing that resists a push or pull. Many of the world's most amazing structures are bridges—tall, spindly bridges carrying trains hundreds of feet above **gorges,** and slender, graceful bridges sweeping across wide **estuaries.**

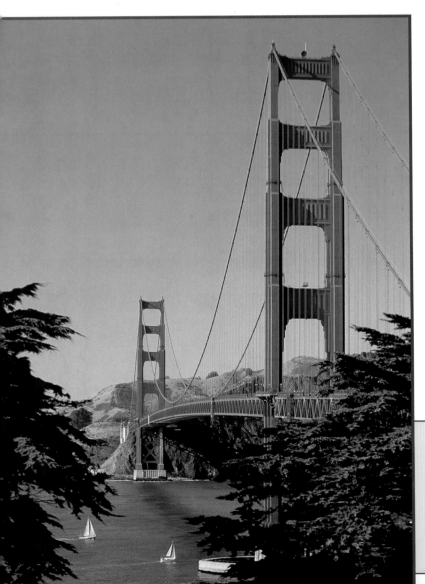

But you also cross hundreds of smaller bridges, which you might not even notice as you speed along in a car or train.

What different types of bridges are there? Who decides where to build them and why? What special materials and machinery are needed?

The Golden Gate Bridge in San Francisco was completed in 1937. The distance between the two towers is 4,200 feet (1,280 meters).

At 160 feet (49 meters) wide, Australia's Sydney Harbor Bridge is the world's widest bridge.

Why do we build bridges?

The main reason for building a bridge is to save time and make transportation more efficient. A long bridge across a river estuary saves a trip on a ferry, or going inland to where the river is narrower. Bridges also allow railroads and fast roads to remain level so trains and vehicles can keep up their speed. Bridges at road and railroad crossings improve safety and reduce jams by avoiding busy intersections.

Types of bridges

Different types of bridges are suitable for different situations, and there are four main types. They are **beam bridges, arch bridges, suspension bridges,** and **cable-stay bridges.** The type used normally depends on the **span**—the distance the bridge must stretch without a support.

FACTS ✤ Bridge world records
- Longest bridge span without support: Akashi Kaikyo suspension bridge, Japan. Length: 6,530 feet (1,990 meters)—nearly 1.25 miles (2 kilometers) without a support! Completed: 1998.
- Longest bridge overall: Second Lake Pontchartrain Causeway, Louisiana. Length: 24 miles (38.4 kilometers). Completed: 1969.
- Highest bridge: Royal Gorge Bridge, Colorado. Height: a dizzying 1,053 feet (321 meters) above river level—the Empire State Building could nearly fit under it! Completed: 1929.

Bridges in the Past

Many thousands of years ago, people made simple log bridges across streams. But the oldest bridges that still survive today are called clapper bridges. They are made of stone slabs supported at their ends by piles of stones. The word "clapper" comes from the Latin word *claprerius,* meaning "pile of stones."

Using the arch

The first long bridges were made of logs joined together to make **beams,** supported on stone **piers.** Long-lasting bridges had to be made of stone, but long stone beams are so heavy that they snap under their own weight. The solution to this problem was the stone arch. Ancient Rome's brilliant **engineers** became experts at building semi-circular stone arches. Their designs were so good that many of their bridges are still in use today, 2,000 years after they were built.

The Pont du Gard in France is still standing, more than 2,000 years after Roman engineers built it.

The Romans also developed simple concrete, which they used in their piers, and the **cofferdam,** which helped them to build piers in the middle of rivers.

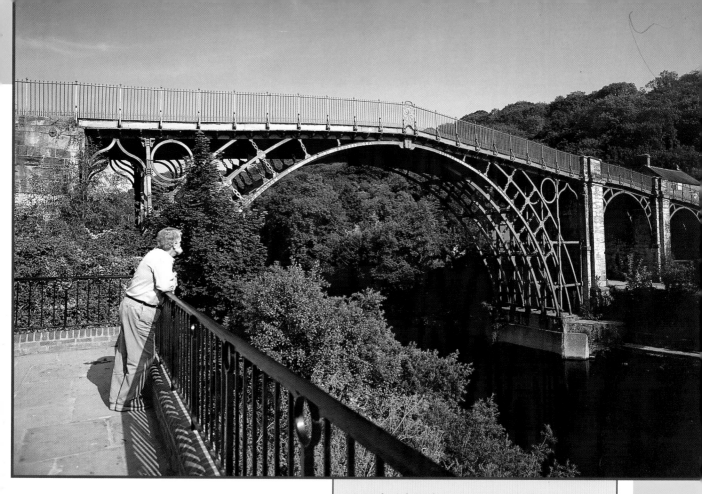

Iron and steel

Ironbridge has spanned the Severn River in England since 1779. It has survived floods that destroyed other bridges on the river.

By the beginning of the 19th century, engineers around the world had figured out how to make long, low stone arches and had built many graceful river bridges. They began using iron for bridge building because iron is stronger than wood and stone. Engineers started designing **arch bridges** made of iron bars and beams, and **suspension bridges** that used iron cables for support. Iron bridges had longer **spans** and were much stronger than the older stone bridges. They were perfect for carrying heavy railroad locomotives over rivers and **gorges.**

Although **steel** is made mostly of iron, it is far stronger than iron alone. Steel took over as the main bridge-building material by the end of the 19th century. It started a new era of bridge building, during which engineers created gigantic **beam bridges** and arch bridges, as well as staggering suspension bridges.

7

Beam Bridges

The simplest type of bridge is just a **beam** supported at each end. A good example is a tree trunk resting on each bank of a stream. The simplest **beam bridge** is a single-**span** bridge, made up of a beam supported by **abutments.** A **cantilever** is a beam supported firmly at just one end. The longer a beam is, the stronger it needs to be, and the heavier it becomes. Beam bridges do not work for spans of more than a few hundred yards because the beams would collapse under their own weight.

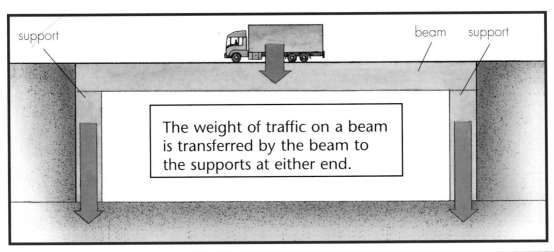

support   beam   support

The weight of traffic on a beam is transferred by the beam to the supports at either end.

beam   abutment

pier

This multiple span bridge has a central **pier**.

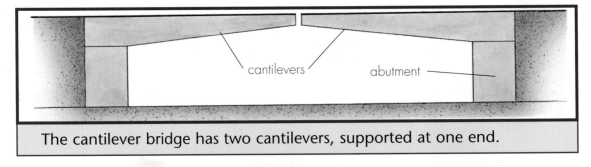

cantilevers   abutment

The cantilever bridge has two cantilevers, supported at one end.

Beams, girders, and trusses

Keep an eye out for different types of beams. Most are made from solid **reinforced concrete. Girders** are made from **steel** plates **welded** together. A **truss** is made by joining together lengths of steel into a framework. A truss can be longer than a girder because it weighs less. One of the first box-girder bridges was the Britannia Bridge in Wales, completed in 1850. Trains actually traveled inside the rectangular girders.

These two truss bridges are in California. The top bridge is a truss arch.

Here are four different kinds of beams.

concrete beam

plate girder (steel)

box girder (concrete)

truss (steel)

TRY THIS

Bending beams

Make a simple beam bridge by supporting a large sponge at each end with books. Press down in the center of the sponge. Can you see that the top part of the sponge is squashed and the bottom part is stretched? The squashed part is in **compression** and the stretched part is in **tension.** This is what happens in a real beam, but a real beam bends much less.

More Bridges

Apart from the various types of **beam bridges,** there are three other types of bridges. They are the **arch bridge,** the **suspension bridge,** and the **cable-stay bridge.**

Curving arches

An arch bridge is supported by an arch-shaped structure that curves upwards between supports at its ends. The weight of the traffic on the bridge is carried around the arch to its ends. Because of its shape, the arch is only in **compression** —the materials in it are squeezed together. There is no **tension,** or pulling apart, at all. This is why arches can be built with stone or brick, which are strong in compression but weak in tension. The ends of the arch push downwards and outwards on its **abutments,** which need to be very strong to keep the ends of the arch from spreading. The biggest arches are massive **steel truss** arches, over 1,640 feet (500 meters) long and as high as a 60-story building.

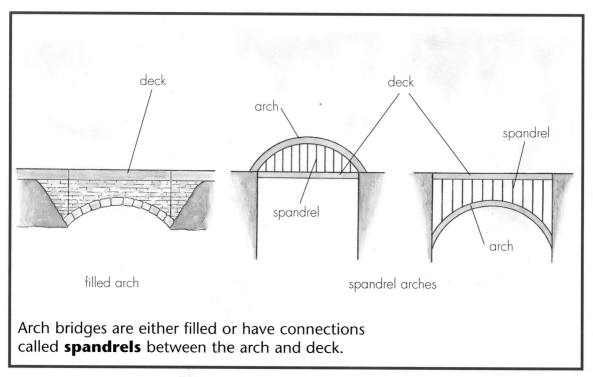

filled arch

spandrel arches

Arch bridges are either filled or have connections called **spandrels** between the arch and deck.

Hanging from cables

Suspension bridges are the giants of the bridge world, with **spans** of 0.6 mile (one kilometer) or more. The world's longest suspension bridge has a main central span of 6,530 feet (1,990 meters). It takes twenty minutes to walk from one support tower to the other! The **deck** that the traffic travels on is suspended on steel cables called **hangers** that are hung across the river or **gorge.** The cables are supported by tall towers, often as high as skyscrapers. The weight of the traffic goes up the hangers, along the cables, down the towers, and also into heavy ground anchors.

The heavy anchors needed to hold the suspension cables can be seen clearly on the Verrazano **Narrows** Bridge in New York.

Cable-stay bridges

Cable-stay bridges are similar to suspension bridges. The deck is held up by cables attached directly to the towers. Cable-stay bridges can have very long spans, but not as long as suspension bridge spans.

Suspended by grass

Simple suspension bridges are made with ropes or wires hung between the banks of rivers. The ropes form handrails, and a simple walkway hangs under them. Before steel cables became easily available, the ropes were made of grass woven together.

Bridge Parts

The various types of bridge look different, but they all have **piers** and **foundations,** which attach the bridges to the ground, and **expansion joints** that allow the parts of a bridge to move slightly. All bridges also have a **deck** along which the traffic moves.

Piers and foundations

A pier is a support that is partway along a bridge. Some piers are made of a single square or circular column. For wide bridges, each pier may be made of two columns with a **beam** across their tops. Piers can be just 12 feet (3.5 meters) high on bridges over roads, or more than 330 feet (100 meters) high on bridges that go over deep valleys. Some long bridges have dozens or even hundreds of piers.

Piers and **abutments** always rest on top of foundations. Foundations carry the huge **loads** of the traffic and hold the bridge itself safely in solid ground, so they often need to be very deep. They keep the bridge from sinking or toppling over.

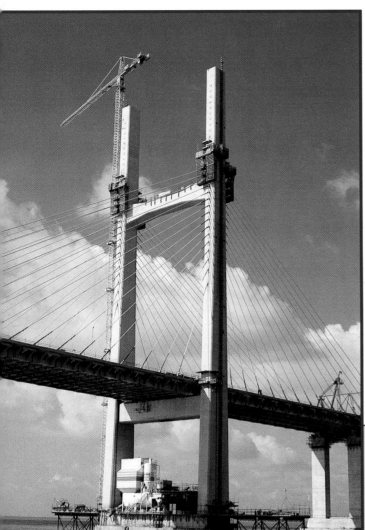

This **cable-stay bridge** has a tower, or pylon, and a pier (right). The road deck is supported by cables.

Allowing for movement

As heavy traffic rolls across a bridge, the parts of the bridge move slightly. For example, in **beam bridges,** the beams sag a tiny bit. Changes of temperature also cause movements. When the temperature rises, the parts of a bridge **expand** slightly. They **contract** when the temperature falls. A rise in temperature of just 36°F (20°C) can cause a 165-foot (50-meter) **steel girder** to grow about 0.4 inch (one centimeter).

Protecting piers

During floods, water flows very quickly around bridge piers in rivers. The piers are designed so that the water flows smoothly around them. This keeps the water from eroding the river bed, which could weaken the piers' foundations. Piers of bridges over busy shipping lanes are protected with barriers in case ships smash into them.

Engineers must allow these movements to happen. If they didn't, unwanted forces would be set up that could eventually break parts of the bridge. Beams rest on **bearing plates** that let the beams move and twist. Gaps are left at the ends of beams to allow for expansion. The gaps are filled with special expansion joints that keep water from leaking into the gaps.

beam

expansion joint

bearing plates

pier

abutment

foundations

This diagram shows bearing plates and an expansion joint on a beam bridge.

Bridge Materials

Wood and stone are useful for making small bridges because they are easy to find and use. But most large bridges today are made from concrete and **steel.**

Steel bridge beams are **prefabricated** from steel plates.

Super-strong steel

Steel is used on its own for **girders, trusses,** and arches, often by **welding** flat steel plates together. It is also used to make cables, **hangers,** and towers for **suspension bridges** and **cable-stay bridges.** Steel is very strong in both **tension** and **compression.** For example, a steel cable as thick as your finger could lift a 30-ton truck.

Pouring concrete

Concrete is another important construction material. It is made up of **cement,** water, and aggregate, which consists of sand and gravel or stone chips. When the ingredients are first mixed, the mixture is runny. Then, when the cement dries and hardens, it binds the sand and gravel together.

Concrete is an excellent construction material because it is quite cheap and immensely strong. In fact, a mug-sized piece of concrete could support a 30-ton truck. It can be set into shapes by pouring it into molds when it is still liquid.

Reinforcing concrete

Concrete is extremely strong in compression. However, in tension it cracks quite easily, so where part of a concrete structure will be stretched, steel is added. This material, made up of concrete and steel bars, is called **reinforced concrete.**

concrete beam

steel bars

In this simple reinforced concrete beam, the steel resists tension in the bottom part of the beam.

Future bridges

It is unlikely that any completely new types of bridges will be developed, but new materials may be used. Extremely long suspension bridges, with **spans** of over a mile, are difficult to build with steel and concrete because of the huge weight. Lighter, stronger materials such as **carbon fiber** and **kevlar** might be used for the **deck** and cables.

Very long concrete **beams** are made with **pre-stressed concrete.** This means that the steel bars in the beam are stretched slightly until the concrete hardens. Then they are released and compress the concrete, giving it extra strength. Pre-stressed concrete beams can be made thinner and lighter than normal reinforced concrete beams.

Designing a Bridge

Before any construction work can begin on a large public bridge, an organization, such as a government transportation department, must decide that a bridge is needed. A **consulting engineer** oversees the design and construction of the bridge for the organization.

New bridges, such as this railroad footbridge, are designed on a computer so that people can see what the bridge will look like before it is built.

What sort of bridge?

The type of bridge depends on its location and how it will be used. Where possible, **beam bridges** with short **beams** and lots of **piers** are chosen because they are easy and cheap to build. But if the water or valley is very deep, piers are difficult to build, so a different type of bridge, such as a **cantilever** or **cable-stay,** is the better choice.

Exploring underground

Geological investigations are made to decide what sort of **foundations** will be needed and to discover any weaknesses in the ground. Rock and soil samples are dug from **boreholes** and tested to see how strong they are.

Designing parts

Next, the **engineers** decide how much weight the bridge must support. They calculate the maximum weight of traffic that is likely to be on the bridge at one time. This is called live **load.** The engineers add this to the weight of the bridge itself, which is called the dead load. They try to keep the dead load as small as possible, to save money and materials, without making the bridge weak.

Against the wind

The sites of long-**span** bridges are often in wide valleys, or near coasts, where the wind can be extremely strong. Bridges must be designed to resist the force of the wind, or else they could collapse. Sometimes they have collapsed! Engineers normally design a bridge to withstand the strongest wind that is likely to happen. In some parts of the world, this can be more than 155 miles (250 kilometers) per hour.

Footbridges often have interesting designs. This one in Uttar Pradesh, India, has cables at each side to keep it from swaying.

Site Preparation

Building a large bridge, such as a **cable-stay bridge** across an **estuary,** is an enormous operation that can take more than five years. Normally one **engineering** company, called the main contractor, is in charge of the whole construction project. Dozens of smaller companies, called sub-contractors, do special jobs such as building cables or **foundations.**

Foundations first

The first stage in building a bridge is to dig holes for the foundations. Powerful earth-moving machines do most of the work. Foundations spread the weight of the bridge and the traffic on it into the ground. The type of foundation chosen depends on what the ground is like. Slab foundations are like rafts that sit on deep, soft ground. **Pile** foundations are used to reach down through shallow soft ground to solid **bedrock.**

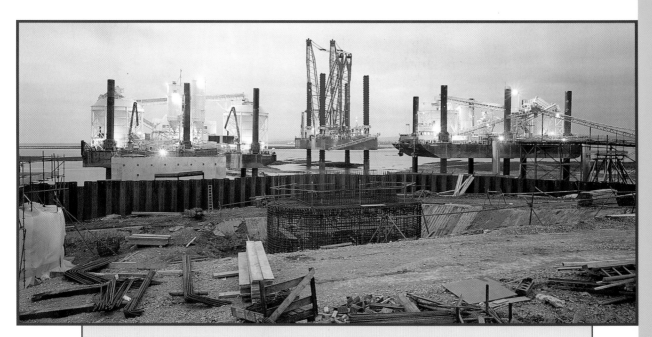

Pier foundations are constructed inside a cofferdam for the Second Severn Crossing between England and Wales.

Cofferdams and caissons

In water, bridge **piers** rest on heavy concrete bases. There are two ways of building these bases. In shallow water, a temporary circular dam called a **cofferdam** is built in the river. The water is pumped out and the soft, **silt** riverbed is dug away until firm ground is found. Then concrete is poured in to make the base. In deep water, the bases are built using **caissons.** A caisson is a **steel** or concrete box with an open base that is dropped to the river bed. Silt is dug out from inside and the caisson sinks until it reaches firm ground. Then it is filled with concrete.

A completed caisson foundation is shown resting on bedrock and filled with concrete.

silt   bedrock

concrete

caisson

TRY THIS

Caissons under pressure

In deep water, **pneumatic** caissons are often used to keep the water from leaking in. Try this experiment to see how they work. Cover the bottom of an empty plastic tub with a layer of sand and fill the tub with water. Cut the base from a small plastic bottle. Place the bottle on the sand and blow gently into the neck. The water will flow out, leaving the sand dry.

blow in here

plastic bottle

tub

water

sand

Building a Beam Bridge

Here you can see how a **beam bridge** is built. The first job is to dig holes for **foundations,** and, if necessary, build **embankments** that take the road at either end of the bridge up to the level of the road **deck.**

Slab foundations

Before any concrete for the foundations is mixed, a mold must be made for it to be poured into. The mold is made with wooden sheets or **steel** plates, called formwork, supported by scaffolding. The reinforcing steel is also put in place so that it will be encased when the concrete sets. The formwork stays in place until the concrete is set.

Piers and beams

Once the concrete in the foundations is set, **piers** and **abutments** are added. These are built in place using more formwork. Short piers are made all at once, but tall piers are made in stages. Concrete is poured into the formwork and is allowed to set. Then the formwork is moved up and more concrete is poured and allowed to set. This continues until the pier reaches its full height.

Reinforced concrete piers are seen here under construction. The right-hand piers have steel formwork in place.

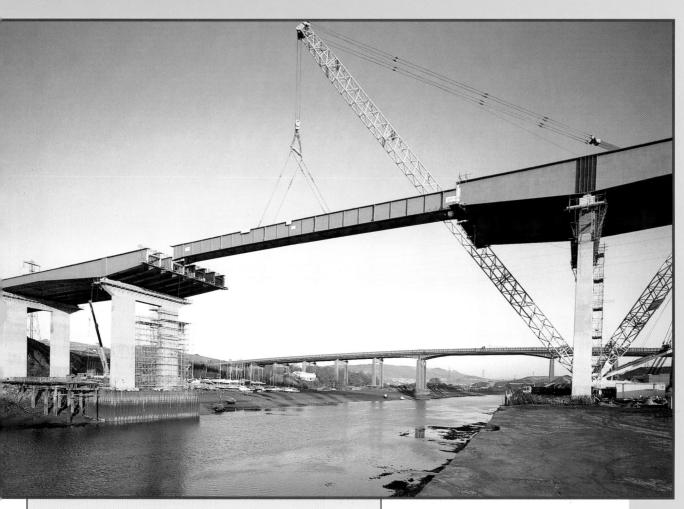

An enormous prefabricated steel beam is lifted into place on a highway bridge.

Bearing plates are placed on the abutments and piers. **Prefabricated** steel **beams** or **pre-cast, pre-stressed** concrete beams are lifted into place. Each **span** is made up of several beams side by side. Formwork is built along the sides, and concrete for the road deck poured. For very short spans a few yards long, concrete beams and slabs are built *in situ,* or on the spot, using formwork. Finally, **expansion joints** are installed.

Building More Bridges

Cable-stay bridges and **suspension bridges** are normally built across wide rivers or between islands, with towers standing in the water.

Foundations and towers

The first stage is to build the **foundations** at the base of each tower using **cofferdams** or **caissons.** The concrete towers are often built by a method called slip-casting. The formwork for the tower gradually creeps upwards. Concrete is poured in the top of the formwork and sets by the time it reaches the bottom.

Suspension cables

Suspension-bridge cables can be more than three feet (one meter) thick. They are made on site by putting hundreds of thin strands of wire next to each other and squashing them together to make the cable. The ends of the cables are connected to heavy ground anchors.

1. Towers built on foundations

tower

foundation

2. Starting at towers, **deck** sections are added one by one

deck

3. Completed bridge

This diagram shows the stages in the building of a cable-stay bridge.

The final section of a cable-stay bridge is dropped into place. A cable will be added to support it.

Adding the deck

Each **prefabricated** section is floated into the river on a barge, lifted into place by a crane, and attached to the suspension cable or tower by a **hanger** or cable. Work normally starts at the towers and progresses outwards to the sides and middle. Each new section is connected to the previous one. On cable-stay bridges, the concrete sections are pulled together with tight **steel** cables. On suspension bridges, the steel sections are **welded** together.

FACTS ✤ That's amazing!
- The Brooklyn Bridge, a suspension bridge in New York, contains 14,300 miles (23,000 kilometers) of wire in its cables. That's enough to stretch more than halfway round the world!
- The **cantilevers** of Scotland's Forth Railway Bridge are made up of 55,000 tons (50,000 metric tons) of steel tubes and **girders.**
- The suspension towers at opposite ends of the Humber Bridge in England are 1.5 inches (4 centimeters) further apart at the top than the bottom, to allow for the curving surface of the earth!

Bridges in Use

Once the structure of a bridge is complete, the bridge is prepared for use. The road surface is laid down on top of the road **deck** and road markings are painted on it. Safety fencing is put up along the sides of the bridge to keep vehicles from skidding off in an accident. Lighting illuminates the road surface at night. Navigation lights are also added to **piers** in water to warn ships, and to the top of towers to warn aircraft.

Many large road bridges are toll bridges, which drivers have to pay to cross. The tolls help to pay for the construction and maintenance of the bridge. Often a row of toll booths is built at one end of the bridge, where drivers can pay their toll without getting out of their vehicles.

London's famous Tower Bridge is a lifting or "bascule" bridge. Every so often, traffic stops so that the bridge can open to allow tall ships to pass underneath.

Bridge maintenance

A bridge needs to be maintained properly. **Steel** bridges are painted regularly to protect them from being damaged by chemical reactions with the air and water. Concrete and steel parts must be checked for cracks. Cracks in concrete can let water reach the reinforcing steel inside. Tiny cracks in steel can spread, weakening the bridge. Older bridges often need to be strengthened to keep them from collapsing under the weight of heavy modern trucks.

In bad weather

Bridges are designed to stand up to high winds, but the winds can be dangerous for the traffic on them. When it is windy, speed limits slow vehicles down. High-sided vehicles, such as buses and trailers, may not be allowed to cross in case a gust flips them over! In very strong winds the bridge may be closed completely.

Instant bridges

Rivers are major obstacles for armies, especially when permanent bridges are destroyed. Army **engineers** build temporary bridges called Bailey bridges after their inventor, Sir Donald Bailey. Some come in parts that must be assembled. Others unfold from the back of special vehicles.

This Bailey bridge carries a road over a stream that has washed away the original bridge.

Bridge Disasters

Modern bridges are designed to withstand heavy traffic, bad weather, floods, and earthquakes. But bridges cannot stand up to unexpected events. They can be destroyed in flash floods and big earthquakes. The worst disasters happened in the past, before **engineers** fully understood structures and the materials they were using. Things can also go wrong as a bridge is built. Small mistakes in the design or unexpected rocks under the ground can delay building and increase the cost of the finished bridge.

This Japanese expressway toppled sideways during the 1995 earthquake in Kobe, Japan. The piers did not have enough reinforcing **steel** to be able to withstand the quake.

Collapse on the Tay

The Tay Bridge in Scotland, built in the 1870s, was an iron **truss** supported on dozens of tall iron **piers.** On a stormy night in December 1879, the central section of the bridge collapsed into the River Tay as a train crossed. Seventy-five passengers died. The poor-quality, brittle iron had cracked because of the sideways force of the wind on the trusses.

Bridge twister

The most famous bridge collapse happened at Tacoma **Narrows** in Washington state in 1940. A new **suspension bridge** had just been completed, designed to withstand winds of more than 125 miles (200 kilometers) per hour. In a wind of just 47 miles (75 kilometers) per hour, the **deck** began to move wildly up and down and twist from side to side. Eventually it broke up and fell into the river below. Fortunately no one was killed or injured. Engineers realized that the deck was not stiff enough, and the wind had been just the right speed to make it vibrate. Decks on similar bridges were quickly stiffened.

Building problems

In the past, safety on building sites was not as good as it is now. Many workers died during the construction of bridges. The worst place to work was in **pneumatic caissons,** such as the ones used to build the **foundations** of the Brooklyn Bridge (1869–1883). Many workers suffered from a condition known as the "bends" because of the sudden reduction in air pressure as they came out of the caissons. At the time nobody understood what caused the bends. Hundreds of workers were crippled, and three died.

Bridge Facts

FACTS ✛ Longest spans—suspension bridges

BRIDGE	(FEET)	(METERS)	COMPLETED
Akashi Kaikyo, Japan	6,530	1,990	1998
Great Belt Link, Denmark	5,330	1,624	1997
Humber, England	4,625	1,410	1981
Tsing Ma, Hong Kong, China	4,520	1,377	1977
Verrazano **Narrows**, WA	4,260	1,298	1964
Golden Gate, CA	4,200	1,280	1937

FACTS ✛ Longest spans of each type of bridge

TYPE	BRIDGE	FEET	METERS	COMPLETED
Arch	New River Gorge, WV	1,700	518	1977
Beam	Rio Niteroi, Brazil	985	300	1974
Cable-stay	Tatara, Japan	2,920	890	1999
Cantilever	Pont de Québec, Canada	1,800	549	1917
Suspension	Akashi Kaikyo, Japan	6,530	1,990	1998

The Humber Bridge, in the north of England, has the world's third longest central span at 4,625 feet (1,410 meters).

The Great Belt Link Bridge in Denmark has the world's tallest bridge towers, at 833 feet (254 meters), and the second longest main span.

FACTS ✢ Groundbreaking bridges

- 19 B.C. Pont du Gard **aqueduct,** France. Three-tiered Roman aqueduct.
- A.D. 610 Great Stone Bridge, China. Early flattened arch.
- 1779 Ironbridge, England. First iron bridge.
- 1883 Brooklyn Bridge, New York. First **suspension bridge** with **steel** cables.
- 1884 Garabit Viaduct, France. Early long-**span** iron arch.
- 1849 Britannia Bridge, Wales. First box-**girder** bridge.
- 1874 Eads Bridge, St. Louis. First steel **truss** bridge.
- 1890 Forth Railway Bridge, Scotland. First steel **cantilever** bridge.
- 1930 Salginatobel Bridge, Switzerland. Early **reinforced concrete** arch.
- 1931 George Washington Bridge, New York-New Jersey. First very long span suspension bridge.
- 1956 Stromsund Bridge, Sweden. Early **cable-stay bridge.**

FACTS ✢ More types of bridge

- Transporter bridge: A bridge that carries passengers or vehicles across a river in a cage, similar to a cable car.
- Pontoon bridge: A **beam bridge** in which the **beams** are supported by pontoons—flat-bottomed boats—on water.
- Habitable bridge: A bridge that supports houses and offices as well as a road **deck.**
- Aqueduct: A bridge that carries a water channel, such as a canal.

Glossary

abutment   support at the end of a bridge

aqueduct   bridge that carries a water channel

arch bridge   bridge supported by one or more arch-shaped structures

beam   long piece of wood or metal that spans an opening and supports a structure above

beam bridge   bridge made up of a beam supported at its two ends

bearing plate   plate between a beam and a pier that allows the beam to bend and slide slightly

bedrock   hard, solid rock deep underground

borehole   deep, narrow hole bored down into the ground to take samples of the earth and rocks below

cable-stay bridge   bridge with a deck supported from above by cables attached to towers

caisson   large steel or concrete box that is sunk into water and filled with concrete to form a foundation

cantilever   beam supported at only one end

canyon   steep-sided rocky valley

carbon fiber   light, strong material made from fibers of carbon

cement   mixture of chemicals that hardens into a rock-like substance after it is mixed with water

cofferdam   temporary dam that keeps water from flowing into excavations during construction work

compression   state of being pressed or squeezed together

consulting engineer   engineer who decides how a structure should be built, rather than an engineer who builds it

contract   to become smaller

deck   part of a bridge on which traffic travels

embankment   bank with a flat top and sloping sides. It is built by piling up earth and rock.

engineer   person who designs or builds a structure

estuary   wide, tidal section of a river, where it meets the sea

expand   to get larger

expansion joint   flexible rubber joint between two beams that allows them to expand and contract slightly

foundation   structure that spreads the weight of a bridge and the traffic on it into the ground

geological   to do with the rocks that make up the earth

girder beam made of steel plates welded together

gorge deep, narrow, steep-sided rocky valley

hanger steel bar or cable that ties a suspension bridge deck to the cable above

kevlar synthetic fiber that is much stronger than steel wire

load force that presses on a bridge, such as the weight of traffic

narrows narrow channel connecting two bodies of water

pier vertical support part of the way along a bridge

pile long steel or concrete pole driven deep into the ground

pneumatic operated by air

pre-cast concrete concrete that is shaped before it is put in place

prefabricated made from parts built in a factory

pre-stressed concrete type of reinforced concrete in which the steel is stretched before concrete is added

reinforced concrete concrete that contains steel reinforcing bars

silt very fine soil washed down a river and deposited at its mouth

span section of a bridge between two supports, the distance between two supports, or the overall length of a bridge

spandrel vertical support that connects an arch to the road deck held up by the arch

steel type of very strong metal made mostly of iron

suspension bridge bridge with a deck that is supported from above by a cable stretched between the ends of the bridge

tension state of being pulled apart

truss beam made of a framework of lengths of steel or wood

weld to attach two pieces of metal to each other by heating them until they melt, then joining them together

More Books to Read

Johmann, Carol, Elizabeth Rieth, and Michael P. Kline. *Bridges!: Amazing Structures to Design, Build & Test.* Charlotte, Vt.: Williamson Publishing Company, 1999.

Kaner, Etta. *Bridges.* Niagara Falls, N.Y.: Kids Can Press, Limited, 1994.

Ricciuti, Edward R. *America's Top 10 Bridges.* Woodbridge, Conn.: Blackbirch Press Incorporated, 1997.

Index